THEIR JOURNEY TO THE PHD:

My Sisters Stories of Becoming Scholar Practitioners, Volume 2

Edited by
Amina M. Abdullah-Winstead, PhD

Copyright © 2014 Amina M. Abdullah-Winstead.

All Rights Reserved. Except as permitted under the U.S. Copyright Act of 1976, no part of this publication may be reproduced, distributed, transmitted in any form or by any means, or stored in a database or retrieval system, without the prior written permission of the publisher.

Hawthorne Press
289 Jonesboro Rd
Suite 160
McDonough, GA 30253
Email: hawthornepub@gmail.com

First Print Book Edition: January 2014
ISBN-10: 0985431652
ISBN-13: 978-0-9854316-5-5

Library of Congress Control Number: 2014930396

Dedication

I dedicate this book to words of wisdom and inspiration of my grandmothers Hameeda Abdullah aka Fodi Arnette (deceased) for saving spare change in a coffee for the education of her grandchildren, Maneera Deen (deceased) for providing funds to keep the dream alive, and my dear friend Stacey L. Robertson (deceased). Like many single moms, Stacey wanted more out of life. She worked fulltime, maintained a household, and attended college as a fulltime student. Their stories of perseverance and pushing forward helped shape me into the woman that I am. Thank you.

Acknowledgments

Wendy Seay Oliver, Ph.D., Quenika Boston, Ph.D., Patricia Bailey, Ph.D., Arlene Peters, Ph.D., Jackie E. Smalls, Ph.D., and Renita L. Webb, Ph.D., thank you for volunteering for this project and sharing your stories. You lead first by example! The successful completion of your doctoral degree shows the desire, dedication, and determination that one can put fourth when he or she believes in his or her self.

Table of Content

1. ACKNOWLEDGMENTS — vi
2. CHAPTER 1: WENDY SEAY OLIVER, PhD — 1
3. CHAPTER 2: QUENIKA BOSTON, PhD — 6
4. CHAPTER 3: PATRICIA BAILEY, PhD — 12
5. CHAPTER 4: ARLENE PETERS, PhD — 20
6. CHAPTER 5: JACKIE E. SMALLS, PhD — 29
7. CHAPTER 6: RENITA L. WEBB, PhD — 39
8. ABOUT THE EDITOR — 52

Wendy Seay Oliver, Ph.D.

The completion of my doctorate degree was the culmination of a hard, long, and trying journey that had been set as a goal in my youth. I can recall as a straight "A" student in elementary school earning the right to speak at an Honor's assembly. At the end of my speech, I announced, "When I grow up, I want to be a doctor with my own business". The crowd burst into a rousing applause. Although I didn't quite understand the magnitude of my goal, the bar had been set.

I was blessed to grow up with two parents that provided all of my needs and instilled tons of confidence in me. I grew up with a big brother that was always encouraging, and served as a built in best friend. I was raised in a neighborhood that was truly a village where everyone looked out for each other. Needless to say, I had an amazing upbringing filled with love and much family support from grandparents, aunts, uncles, cousins, and family friends. It wasn't until much later (when I attended graduate school on a minority grant) that I realized I was a minority (African American and a woman) that was not supposed to have big dreams and family support.

I maintained Honor Roll status throughout elementary, middle, and high school while also devoting most of my time to performing with competitive baton twirling. Through competitive baton twirling, I learned that practice, hard work, and perseverance were required to reach your aspirations. Upon graduating from North Clayton High School, I was fortunate to earn an academic and performance scholarship to pursue my undergraduate degree in Speech Language Pathology at South Carolina State University.

During my college years while maintaining Honor Roll status, my focus was more on University campus life. Most of my time was consumed with practicing for weekly performances as a feature baton twirler and Champagne dancer for the Marching "101" Band. My energy was also consumed with pledging the internationally renowned sorority of Delta Sigma Theta Incorporated. It wasn't until my senior year in college that my focus shifted back to my academic goals and the impact I would have on others through my profession. After graduation, I was all set to return to my hometown of Atlanta, GA and obtain my Master's degree so that I could continue my quest to become a licensed speech therapist; however, God had other plans.

I was very disappointed that my hometown had limited speech language pathology graduate programs and only accepted 10% of applicants, while also giving priority to their own undergraduate students. I received the "please try again next semester letter" from both of the graduate programs that I applied and was very disappointed. Basically, my professional goals seemed as if they were being detoured. I began frantically applying for any and every graduate school still accepting applications, and subsequently found the University of the District of Columbia that had a grant from the National Institutes of Health (NIH) that was looking for minority research assistants like me. This research assistant position that I was awarded for graduate school ignited my passion for research and specifically helped me grow a deeper appreciation for my culture, history, and those that are born disenfranchised.

During my graduate years, I learned that most minority communities were underserved due to the underrepresentation of medical professionals within the community. Lack of professionals results in less than optimal treatment, and denies individuals the personalized attention afforded to those in other communities. I realized cultural barriers can still segregate individuals from specialty care, and treatments that are not geared to meet their hereditary needs. It was during this time that I pledged I would go back into the minority communities upon graduating and not only work within the underserved communities, but also provide research to assist in closing the healthcare gap that exists. I enjoyed my graduate school years in Washington, DC and felt that I not only grew as a student, but as a person. I graduated with honors and returned to Atlanta with everything I needed to be a licensed speech therapist.

My first year out of school, I returned to Atlanta from completing school in Washington, DC and was offered a job in a lucrative rehabilitation clinic. I loved my job and helping people, but I never forgot my promise that I would return and help the minority community. During this time, I got married. With the security of health benefits from my husband, I decided to leave my salary position and go for it as an independent speech therapist contractor. My coworkers were sad to see me leave, and warned me of leaving a stable job. However, I proceeded forward and began serving children within minority communities. Just as research had taught me, the minority community was so underserved that I quickly grew a full caseload and eventually had more clients than I could handle. I started bringing in subcontractors, and today I have a successful private practice- Outspoken Therapy Services, Inc.

My priorities shifted as my children were born, and I placed professional/educational goals on hold. During this time, I began working a part-time schedule to spend time with my babies and hired more speech therapists to cover the company's growing caseload. As my youngest child became ready to enter preschool, I contemplated resuming working a regular 40 hour week when my cousin mentioned she was beginning a program with an online University to obtain her doctorate degree. My initial goal that I had made as a child was to become a doctor, and this seemed like the perfect opportunity. I decided to make a call to Capella University for more information, and by the time I had gotten off the phone I had started the application process to begin my doctoral journey.

I was excited about beginning my PhD program. I thought I had my schedule mapped out so that I had the perfect balance between family, work, and school. I would work 2.5 days a week, go to school 2.5 days a week, and devote my evening and weekends strictly to family. I was in for a rude awakening. I realized I had been away from school for 10 years and forgot the stress that studying, completing assignments, and writing papers with deadlines placed on your life. Coupled with the fact that I now had family and work responsibilities there were many times that I felt I had made the wrong decision. Being that I was determined not to take time away from my family, there were many nights that I would get up once everyone was sound asleep to complete assignments and research papers. Needless to say, there were many mornings that I started the day exhausted, and felt I needed to place my PhD journey on hold. With lots of support from family and friends, prayer, and God's strength, I finished!! I will never forget the words when my PhD committee said, "Congratulations Dr, you successfully defended your dissertation!!" I hope that every individual can experience the elation of speaking a lifetime goal into existence. My wish for African Americans and little girls of all racial backgrounds is that no societal barrier keeps you from losing focus of your goals and dreams. Dreams can become reality with hard work, perseverance, commitment, and faith if you believe in yourself first. Dr. Wendy Seay Oliver CCC-SLP

Quenika Boston, Ph.D.

My name is Quenika Boston and I completed my PhD at Capella University. Obtaining my PhD was something I never planned to do when I started my college journey. It was a long road, but I made it. First, let me give you a little background about me and who I am. I am 35 years old, was born in Miami, FL, and is considered by my family (primarily my mother) a miracle child. I was born with Congenital Heart Disease and was deemed not to live past 18 years old unless I had open-heart surgery. I was born with four holes in my heart and without a pulmonary valve. At the age of four, I had my first open heart surgery where they patched the holes in my heart.

During that time, early 80s, technology was not as advanced as it is now, so my mom elected to wait to have a pulmonary valve put in because it would have been artificial and would need to be replaced every ten years. At age 12, I was blessed to have what the medical field calls a homograph, or a human pulmonary valve put in. A young boy died and he was a donor, so I received his pulmonary valve. That was my second open-heart surgery. Throughout my heart condition, I also developed Scoliosis, the curvature of the spine. By the age of 14, the curve in my spine was so severe that a brace would not be effective. Therefore, I had to have spinal surgery where my spine was straightened and two steel rods (one on each side of my spine) were placed in my back. This was a very difficult surgery due to the pain but I pushed through. I recovered well and continued to live life as a normal teenager. At the age of 20, I developed an infection from the rods, which required another back surgery to remove the rods. I still have slight Scoliosis, but the rods fused the spine well and my spine has not begun to curve anymore. Being as though I was the only child, and my mother was raising me as a single mother, my medical conditions made us very close.

Even through all of that, education was a high priority in my mom's household. According to my mom's standards, I could not have anything less than a B on my report card. Anything less was unacceptable. I thought this was a little harsh, but my mom knew my potential. However, I too felt that education was important and always strived to do my best, well...most of the time. I maintained a 3.4 GPA throughout high school and graduated top ten percent in my class. I then enrolled in Morris Brown College (MBC) at the age of 18. I attended MBC for two years and did nothing but party! My conduct showed that I was not ready to leave home. I did not have the discipline to attend class and virtually live on my own. As a result, during my sophomore year, I dropped out of school and returned home. I took classes at the local community college and worked so I could contribute around the house. It was not until I met my wife that I refocused on school.

In 2001, I moved to California with my partner and it was there where I made the conscious decision to start my college journey over. I started over at Solano Community College, earned my Associate Degrees in Social Science and Liberal

Arts. I transferred to the University of Phoenix and earned my Bachelor's Degree in Human Services. At this point, my mom started calling me a career student. She thought that was funny, but so did I. I began to work in the field of Human/Social Services and quickly realized that I needed more than a Bachelor's degree. University of Phoenix did not have a Master's Degree program in Human Services, which led me to earning my Master's in Human Services at Capella University. I do not know what possessed me to enroll in the PhD program, but I did. Still maintaining my "career student" status, I embarked on my PhD journey in the fall of 2008.

My mom, who always has my back and my wife, who also always has my back; they encouraged and supported me throughout my PhD. Without their support and encouragement, I probably would have quit the program. Due to my mom's educational standards when I was a child, I became a stickler about my grades. I maintained a 4.0 GPA throughout my Master's program as well as the PhD program. Completing the coursework part of the PhD program was an easy feat. The challenges came when I started the dissertation process. Completing the Scientific Merit Review (SMR) was the most frustrating part of the process. It took me three quarters, yes three, to get the SMR approved! My mentor and committee members were supportive throughout the process, but receiving the constant requests for changes became frustrating. In addition, two of my committee members changed in the middle of my SMR review which somewhat started the review process over. My mentor would not respond in a timely manner due to technical issues on her part. What just seemed like issue after issue kept occurring. I eventually had a conference call with my mentor and committee members to ensure we were all on the same page and to inform them that I only had three more quarters to complete my PHD program because I was reaching my lifetime maximum for financial aid. In addition, I got my advisor involved who helped light a fire under my mentor's butt!

Once I finally got past the SMR process, it went fairly smooth. I still had some hang-ups though. My proposal was complete by the time the school approved my SMR. However, in December 2010, I began to feel shortness of breath along with experiencing other symptoms that prompted me to see my Cardiologist. I was told in January 2011 that after 21 years of my pulmonary valve being implanted, it had worn out and was no longer functioning, as it should. Thus, I needed to have a pulmonary valve replacement. In August 2011, I flew to Miami, FL from Atlanta, GA to have a pulmonary valve replacement; this time, with an artificial valve. Due to the advances in medicine, I did not have to have open-heart surgery. They were able to replace the valve through a catheter and I was only in the hospital for a day. Meanwhile, my proposal was still in the review process and was now at the committee review stage. In November, I began to feel ill and went to see my Cardiologist here in Atlanta. During my visit, the doctor indicated that I had an infection, which resulted in my immediate admission into the hospital. I had Endocarditis, an infection from the artificial valve as well as a Pulmonary Embolism (a blood clot in my lungs). I was hospitalized during the Thanksgiving holiday for two and a half weeks. Upon release, I had to remain home for four more weeks with a PICC-line in my arm to continue with the antibiotics.

During my time home, I continued to work on my proposal all while still facing challenges with the school. Once my committee approved my proposal, the school deferred it requesting additional changes. I made the changes, and my mentor resubmitted the new proposal. The school deferred it again stating that I did not make any changes. It was then discovered that the school reviewer was looking at the wrong proposal, which took another two weeks out of the quarter. By this time, it was the spring of 2012 and it was my last quarter of financial aid. I was starting to stress out because I did not know if I would be able to finish my PhD program. I finally got school and IRB approval (that took a couple of submissions as well) and was able to move on to data collection. Data collection went pretty smoothly and I completed my full dissertation by September. With the help of my wonderful advisor and admission from my mentor of all of the delays on her and the school's behalf, I was able to get some tuition refunded. Moreover, even though I cannot state what exactly took place to get me to the end of my program, let's just say that Capella wanted to see me complete my PhD program and that is what I did.

No, I did not start my college career with the goal of obtaining my PhD and becoming Dr. Quenika Boston. However, I had a strong mom who taught me that education was valuable and wanted me to reach higher than what she did. I had plenty of people that supported me beyond just my mom and wife. My supervisor (and friend) at work supported me and I even encouraged her to enroll into the PhD program at Capella (she could probably kill me now though). My friends, other family members, and the PhD Sisters Group all helped me get through this journey. It took me to use all of my lifetime loan money through financial aid and even some monetary support from my wife and mom, but I made it. Most importantly, it was God and my faith in Him that ultimately led me to complete this journey. Although it was a challenging road, I am glad that I decided to travel down this road, which was bumpy at times, but eventually evened out. In addition, it sure does feel good to be called Dr. Boston, or what I prefer to be called, Dr. Que. I am the first in my family to become a doctor and they are so proud of me. I am proud of me. I am a proud African American woman who became a doctor after facing so many challenges in my life. If you stay grounded, humbled, focused, motivated, and faithful, you too can be the first in your family to become a doctor.

Patricia Bailey, Ph.D.

This journey would definitely be a big step for me. I battled many thoughts and emotions. But before I share my doctoral journey, I must I would like to briefly share a personal story that lead up to my doctoral journey. I was late going to college. After high school, I decided to get married, work and have children. Although, I always had a good job, I struggled financially as my first husband was not a provider. I was the sole breadwinner of the family. It was not until ten years had passed by that I realized that I needed an education if I wanted to succeed in life. I knew it would be hard as I had a family and needed to work. I was not sure how supportive my husband would be about my decision to return to school. I prayed about it and in January 2003, I enrolled in a local community college to pursue an Associate Degree in Nursing. Seven months prior to completing my Associate Degree, my then non-supportive husband decided to walk out on our four children and me. I was devastated. However, I knew I had to finish the race, which I did in May 2003. I accepted a full time nursing position at a large teaching hospital in Ohio. I moved my girls to a new state for a fresh start.

Honestly, I had no desire to pursue an education beyond my Associate Degree. I was content. God had answered my prayers to allow me to get an education. I worked for one and half years and for some odd reason, I had the desire to go back to school. Not really sure why but I followed and enrolled in a Registered Nurse (RN) to Bachelors of Science degree in Nursing (BSN) program in January of 2005. The classes were one day a week. As a new single mother, I worked three twelve hour shifts, went to school one day, and managed to continue to provide for and support my daughters. During my time in this program, I met a wonderful God-fearing man. He supported my educational journey and assisted me with my daughters. He was also a single parent raising two small daughters of his own. I was able to complete the program in four semesters to earn my Bachelor's Degree in Nursing in May 2006; however, I was not able to attend graduation as I had unexpectedly lost a brother from a heart attack. Even in my time of sorrow, I rejoiced in the Lord.

Very shortly after completing my Bachelor's Degree in Nursing, I had a desire to go further. I am now thinking to myself, what is really going on. I am satisfied with where I am in life. I have a supportive companion, wonderful daughters, and a great job. I questioned why I needed to get another degree. I stop questioning these thoughts and feelings and three months after completing my BSN, I enrolled in a Master's of Nursing program with a specialty in family nurse practitioner. I completed this program in seven quarters and graduated June 2008. During my time in this program, my supportive companion proposed and we were married September 2008. After passing my certification exam to practice as a nurse practitioner, I had a hard time finding a nurse practitioner job as a new graduate. However, there was a strong need for nursing faculty. I accepted a full time faculty job at a local nursing college. Within the first three months of teaching, I realized that I actually love teaching and helping future nurses to achieve their dream. Two co-workers and I decided to pursue our doctoral degree in nursing education together. I must admit that I was excited and nervous at the same time. I wondered if my new husband would support the idea of me pursuing a fourth degree in addition to how my children would react to the news that their mother decided to go back to school again.

After a family discussion, fast, and pray, I enrolled at Capella University. My first quarter started December 2008. I was so excited about my new educational journey. However, two weeks into the quarter, my mother passed away. I was devastated. I made it successfully through the first quarter but not with the grade that I wanted. Therefore, I decided to take the next quarter off to grieve. Well, the next quarter eventually turned into me taking 3 quarters off. In the summer of 2009, I saw the following scripture multiple times in one week: "For I know the plans I have for you, plans to prosper you and not to harm you, plans to give you hope and a future"- Jeremiah 29:11. I now know why I always had a desire to continue my education beyond my Associate Degree. God was preparing me for something to come. It was time for me to get back on the path. I re-enrolled in the fall of 2009 and completed all of the required coursework by the spring of 2011. I successfully passed my Comprehensive Exam during the summer of 2011 and entered into the dissertation phase fall of 2011.

At the start of the dissertation phase, I was excited. I had 16 milestones to complete. Prior to starting my dissertation quarter, I had already completed milestones 1 and 2 (Committee Approval and Completion of CITI modules).

Although I had a long way to go, I felt like I was almost at the finish line. However, at the first conference call with my Mentor, I learned that my topic was not an education focus. My mentor was wonderful as she helped me to fine-tune my topic to where I was still able to keep part of the focus but the topic would be more and educational rather than clinical. I was still discouraged and ultimately ended up wasting an entire quarter, as I did not accomplish anything. During my course work, I wrote papers on the topic that I had hoped to reference when working my dissertation. I had a vast amount of literature on the topic, but I needed to collect more information for the literature review. It was like starting over. Furthermore, I felt alone on my dissertation journey. However, I was not alone. I still had my supportive family, my church family cheering me on, and my friends.

One day, something fascinating happened. Another doctoral learner at the time, added me to the PhD sister group on Facebook. As I would read everyone's struggles and success, I realized that what I am going through is part of the process. I must go through this process to get my results. The following quarter, I was more motivated than ever. By the end of January 2012, I completed milestone 3 (Mentor Approved Proposal). At this point, I hit a roadblock. I was awaiting committee approval. One committee member had approved my dissertation with no corrections or editing within the schools' required time frame. My second committee was missing in action. My advisor and my mentor sent numerous emails and this committee member would not respond. I was angry and discouraged at the same time.

During this time, I was reminded of a book that I had read by Bruce Wilkinson, David and Heather Kopp titled

"The Dream Giver". The book is about following your God given destiny. It starts with a parable of an individual named "Ordinary" who starts to embrace his big dream. Before he starts on his journey, he leaves his comfort zone. I left my comfort zone in 2008 when I started on my doctoral journey. After leaving his comfort zone, Ordinary meets bullies at the borderline. I felt the bullies I met on the way were people who did reach their success and were trying to discourage me from reaching mine. Most of these people where co-workers. In the parable, after getting past the bullies, Ordinary enters the wasteland. I entered a wasteland after my mother passed away. However, God showed me that He has never left or forsaken me. Ordinary soon finds sanctuary. Ironically, I found my sanctuary with my PhD sisters. The PhD Sisters Group in addition to other doctoral support groups became my rock of support, my sanctuary. The sanctuary is an oasis that transforms the individual. If anybody could understand what I was going through, they could. After sitting at a standstill for one quarter, I was able to pick up where I left off and start on the journey again.

Returning by to the parable, after leaving the sanctuary to continue on his journey, Ordinary entered the 'Valley of Giants'. The giants were on the path to block Ordinary from continuing on his journey. I felt like I entered the 'Valley of Giants' at several points on the path of completing my dissertation journey. I met the first giant at milestone 3 when one of the committee members was missing. My mentor along with one committee member had approved my dissertation January 2012. The month of February was a waste as we waited on the other committee member. After my advisor and mentor had sent several emails with no result, they partitioned on my behalf for a new committee member. I received a new and awesome committee member within 48 hours. I completed milestone 4 on March 9, 2012.

I set out on my journey again. At this point, I am happily traveling along my path having completed milestones 5, 6, and 7 (School Approval, Institutional Review Board (IRB) Approval, and Completion of Pre-data Conference Call) by May 2012, when I meet yet another giant. This giant was bigger than any giant I had encountered on my dissertation journey. Shortly after I received approval to start collecting data, I received a notification that I no longer had any financial aid left to fund the remainder of my education. Not only was I out of funds, but I also needed to cover the prior quarter's tuition. Once again, I was devastated. Because of the cost of my doctoral education, we were already living paycheck to paycheck. I did not know where I was going to get money to pay for the previous quarter or future quarters.

During this time of devastation, I consulted once again with my PhD Sisters who informed me to apply for a graduate plus loan. This loan is based on your credit. When I first applied, I was denied. I have the heart of a warrior. I knew I had to do something to defeat the giants in my path. After all, I had already defeated one earlier. I later found out there was an old collection on my credit. After researching the debt and working with the collection agency, I settled the account. I reapplied for the graduate plus loan and was approved. I received enough funds to cover the prior quarter's tuition as well as tuition for the next fiscal school year.

From June to the end of July 2012, I collected data and wrote Chapters 4 and 5 of my dissertation. By the end of August, my mentor and committee had approved both chapters. This was the completion of Milestones 8, 9 and 10 (Mentor Approval of chapter 4, Mentor Approval of Chapter 5 and Full Dissertation and Committee Approval of Dissertation). I was over joyed. I could not believe that this was happening. I am almost at the finish line. So far, I had defeated the borderline bullies, survived the wasteland, found my sanctuary oasis, and defeated two giants. Was this just a dream or was my dream becoming a reality. I received school approval September 2012 (Milestone 11), followed by format editing completion (Milestone 12) in middle of October 2012. I successfully defended my dissertation October 24, 2012 and my degree was conferred on October 31, 2012 (Milestone 13). Completion of the final three milestones did not require my involvement.

As I look back, I expected the journey of my dream to look and appear differently. Just like Ordinary in the parable, when I began to feel that my dream was finally accomplished, the Dream Giver whispered and said, "Let me show you more". Achieving your dream, successful completion of your doctoral education and dissertation is only the beginning. For me, it was the beginning of a new start in more ways than one. I realized that all the hurdles and roadblocks that I encountered were preparation for the bigger things God has in store for me. I am currently Sunday School Superintendent of my church, a practicing full-time nurse practitioner, and an online adjunct faculty.

I pray that everyone who reads my journey is able to continue on your own doctoral journey with new strength and confidence. As you begin to embrace your big dream, you will have to be like Ordinary and myself: (1) Embrace your dream of completing your doctoral journey; (2) Leave your comfort zone and stop fearing the unknown; (3) Overcoming the borderline bullies who will try to deter you from starting out of your journey; (4) When you enter the wasteland, no that God is still with you every step of the way; (5) Find a sanctuary in the sisterhood of those who have gone before you and in those who are on the journey with you; (6) When you reach the Valley of Giants (committee members, mentors, financial aid, family, work, etc.) – take on the heart of a warrior and defeat all giants you encounter on the way; (6) finally, live out your big dream. However, know that when you reach your land of promise, it is only the beginning. God bless you all.

Arlene Peters, Ph.D.

I am Arlene Peters, Ph.D. It did not dawn on me until a few years after earning my M.S. that I would return to school to pursue a Ph.D. I made this decision 16 years after earning my M.S. It all began with a reoccurring haunting dream where I had to recomplete either high school or undergrad. Those dreams were extremely vivid. I would find myself in the familiar hallways of my high school campus and while present, I would verbally question myself as to why I was there when I already had a master's degree or a bachelor's degree. I would also see myself on my undergrad campus, walking on the sidewalk close to my old dormitory, questioning why I was back there since I had already earned a master's degree. These dreams lasted for several years. I do not recall when they stopped, but I believe it was when I decided that I was going to return to school to earn my Ph.D. Actually they stopped several years before I returned to grad school.

It was not an easy decision because I did not have the funds, and this was a major concern for my husband. My final decision was made at a women and girls' conference held at the Orlando Convention Center, summer of 2007. It was hosted by Evangelist Juanita Bynum and the title was, "Women on the Frontline". My daughter and I attended and even spent two nights in a local hotel even though we live in Orlando. Evangelist Bynum taught on the topic of "The Treasure within You". Although my memory is a bit faint on all the details of the sermon, I distinctively remember that the overall message was that many women were not using the treasure or all the potential that God had placed in them.

During this message, I was sitting close to some young ladies who appeared to be in their early twenties. I was taking copious notes throughout the sermon. At the end of the sermon, the young ladies and I struck up a conversation. They began to inquire about my profession and seemed to be hungry to find out more about me although I wasn't not sure why. I remember sharing with them that I was a teacher and that I was preparing to go back to school to earn my Ph.D. Since I had been contemplating returning to school before the conference, it seemed like the powerful words by Ms. Bynum and some of the other speakers confirmed what I was planning to do. It was time to pursue that dream in order to get to the next chapter in my life. Although I was not the first in my family to earn a bachelor's degree, I am the first and only to earn a master's and doctoral degree. My paternal grandmother who reared me from 9 months old stressed the importance of education.

Growing up on the island of St. Croix, United States Virgin Islands, the idea of not pursuing a college degree was almost foreign. Post high school, most students either attended the College of the Virgin Islands (CVI) (now the University of the Virgin Islands or UVI) or left to attend college in the United States. I didn't necessarily pay attention to graduate level degrees; however, I knew many local individuals who were medical doctors, lawyers, judges, or working in other professions that required additional education. My grandparents and immediate family members were not professionals, but hard workers nonetheless. My grandmother's youngest brother was a lawyer in New York and although I knew of and about him, I had only met him once in my life. I was the second to last of eight children (cousins, aunts, an uncle, and a sister) within an extended family of 10. Only two of eight children went to college and earned a degree. My cousin, who is five years older than me, earned a bachelor's degree in business administration. I later followed in her footsteps by attending the first year of college at CVI. After spending a year at CVI, I transferred to the University of South Florida, in Tampa to pursue a bachelor's in elementary education. Three years later, I graduated, married, and then started my teaching career. After one year into my career, I returned to college to earn a master's degree in educational leadership. After five years of marriage and having earned my M.S. degree, I started a family. By this time, it was 1993. I focused on child-rearing and my career for the next several years. In 1995, I had my second child. Twelve years later, I enrolled at Capella University. The fact that it was online was extremely appealing to me since my children were in middle school. I could still remain active in their school and extra-curricular activities, teach, and maintain my sanity, or so I thought.

When I started Capella in September of 2007, I took only one course for the first several quarters. It was a very positive experience. Then I added one additional course per quarter-- whoa, what hit me? I became so overwhelmed and discouraged, not so much because I couldn't handle the work load, but because I had a course that left me extremely confused to the extent that I started doubting my ability to complete the program. The following quarter, I ended up taking off the next quarter. Despite earning an "A" in that course, it was not enough reassurance that I was capable of continuing on my doctoral pursuit. I was mentally, emotionally, and physically exhausted. I remember the night prior to resuming my studies; I could barely sleep. I awakened from my sleep and could literally hear my heart pounding. I was perspiring profusely; that's when I realized I was experiencing a major panic attack. I prayed, started taking deep breaths, did some positive self-talk and was eventually able to fall asleep. I awakened to begin the new quarter with two courses, one being statistics. Math is not my strength, but I successfully completed the two courses that quarter.

The rest of my quarters went uneventfully through the comprehensive exam. I passed on the first try and was very pleased with my accomplishment. I had no doubt that I could complete my dissertation. Even with confidence, moral support from family and friends, I hit a boulder! I was repeatedly told that the proposal is an "iterative" process; however, no matter how diligently I tried, I could not complete a proposal that met the satisfaction of my mentor. It appeared that I was consistently receiving messages that were contradictory. Even one of my committee members, a visiting professor, was dumbfounded by what I was requested to change. After I made the requested changes, or wrote exactly what I was told to, I would receive responses that indicated I did not make the changes as recommended.

Nothing I wrote was up to "par". In September of 2009, after the first quarter of my dissertation, I experienced what I now call "mental" paralysis. I could not move forward. I did absolutely nothing during that quarter. The following two quarters, I sank into deep despair and decided to take off the next two consecutive quarters. This actually placed me in the 'not in good standing" status at the university. What happened? During those three quarters, I literally felt like it was over. I prayed, cried, and went into a serious state of depression. I sought the help of those who could help me. Even when they told me that I could and would complete my doctorate, I did not believe them. I had lost all faith in my own abilities to achieve this worthy goal. Why was this? Why did it seem impossible for a doctoral level student, with a 4.0 GPA, to write a quality three-chapter proposal? How was I able to earn a 4.0 GPA throughout my coursework, be specifically told what an excellent job I did on my comps by one of the most respected professors at the university, and yet not be able to write an "acceptable" proposal?

Summer of 2010 rolled around and I mustered up enough faith, strength, and courage to try again. My inspiration came from my sixth grade students' analysis of Langston Hughes' poem, "Dreams", which has now become my favorite:

>Hold onto dreams
>For if dreams die
>Life is a broken-winged bird
>That cannot fly.
>Hold fast to dreams
>For when dreams go
>Life is a barren field
>Frozen with snow.

Amina M. Abdullah-Winstead, PhD

When asked to analyze and interpret the poem, by first identifying the similes and metaphors, my students explained that if a person gives up on her dream, then her life would be empty like an empty field. They further explained that just as a broken-winged bird loses its ability to fly, this causes its life to be hard and limiting, so would life be for the individual who gives up on her dream. Unfulfilled, meaningless, limiting were not the descriptors I wanted for my life.

Both my students' words and the words of this poem haunted me and ultimately propelled me to go after my dream to earn a doctoral degree. So again, I started with the same mentor who was very welcoming and understanding of my situation. Unfortunately, it was notlong before, I started experiencing the same type of contradictory, vague, and confusing requests of changes to my proposal. It was nearing the end of the winter quarter and I knew I had to make a change if I were going to successfully complete my dissertation. After my proposal was *finally* approved in December of 2011, I requested a mentor change.

I started January 2012 with a new mentor, a positive outlook, and a determination to accomplish my goal by December of 2012. I dedicated most of my leisure time during the spring and summer months to completing the Institutional Review Board (IRB) process. I then then took an entire quarter off during which I collected data and wrote my final chapters. On September 11, 2012, I completed my final defense call. My degree was conferred on October 31, 2012. I met and exceeded my goal of completion by December 2012! My dissertation, titled "An Investigation of Teacher Perspectives and Implementation of Differentiated Literacy Instruction with Advanced Students", is published in ProQuest database.

Over the course of my journey there were many lessons learned. A few suggestions are to research doctoral fellowships and scholarships prior to applying to a program, find another doctoral learner who you can work with to complete the journey, and interview at least three potential mentors. Pray and go with the one that you feel most comfortable and supportive. Let him/her know up front your timeline. It is your investment at stake, not theirs. Do not feel guilty if you have to change mentors midstream.

My doctoral buddy was Dr. Tryphene McGee, who I met at my first colloquium. We encouraged and helped each other throughout the entire process. This "accountability partner" need not live in the same state or geographic region. We called each other weekly to share our personal milestones and accomplishments. When she needed someone to field test her instrument, my daughter was an excellent candidate, since she was a first year college student. When I thought that I could go on, Dr. McGee would reassure me that we were both going to make it. When either one of us was stuck on a section of the proposal or on the final leg of the dissertation process, we would exchange ideas or help each other muddle through the fog.

We gave each other tips on meeting our mentors' expectations or assisted each other in interpreting the meaning of their recommendations for change. We discussed our personal and professional goals for the future as Ph.D. sisters. In addition, we shared personal stories and challenges that could potentially hinder our progress and we prayed for each other. Today, we are friends and Ph.D. sisters who will continue to work on reaching our fullest potential.

Enjoy the journey and reward yourself for accomplishing even small personal milestones. Take mental breaks like going to see a good movie or spending time with a friend. Take care of your mental, physical, and spiritual health. At the same time, do not neglect your loved ones to accomplish this goal. Before you earn your degree, during the process, and after you accomplish your goal, they will still be there to love you and support you.

Once you are done with your degree, have a plan for beyond the doctoral journey. Ask yourself if you will be using your degree to advance in your current career, to go into academia or higher education as a professor or administrator, or to start your own business. However, if for some reason, you do not reach or meet your deadline or goal for completion or achievement, remember that the degree does not make you who you are. You are who you are before pursuing this degree. Believe in yourself and love yourself no matter the outcome.

Remember, many successful individuals do not have a doctorate degree. Give yourself the credit for trying. Sadly, know that not everyone will be as happy with your accomplishment as you are. With your new status comes additional responsibility, if given the opportunity to help someone else, do so. Sharing a word of encouragement, taking a few minutes to give advice on the process, as it can make a difference "to whom much is given, is much required" Luke 12:48.

My doctoral journey has truly taught me that anything I consider to be of personal importance and desire to come to fruition in my life is indeed possible. I successfully completed my doctoral program with a 4.0 GPA, my sanity, and yes, unfortunately, a mountain of debt. Meditating on biblical promises was vital to my success. Please permit me to leave you with a few bible verses that have encouraged me along the way, "He, who has begun a good work in you, is faithful to complete it" (Phil. 1:6 NKJV). The other is, "With man, things are impossible, but with God all things are possible" (Matt. 19:26 NKJV).

Jackie E. Smalls, Ph.D.

It was in 2005, when I decided to take the leap to the academic pinnacle towards earning my PhD. I delayed the process just for another year to complete other milestones in my life. The reason I decided to pursue a PhD was because I felt the call to advance my education. In addition, I wanted to enrich my profession with a terminal degree. I felt the PhD would make me more marketable in my field (Organizational Psychology and Development specializing in Leadership). Consequently, I left the US Virgin Islands to advance my education and make a living that would sustain my mother and my children. Nevertheless, cultural stereotypes exist and at times hindered the process, as I will discuss later in this epistle.

Before I decided to enroll in a university, I thought that having your Masters meant that you were respected and understood to have "mastered" your profession. I could not be more wrong. Beginning the summer of 2006, I was examining various online doctoral degree-granting institutions. Because of my daily profession, the only type of degree that would accommodate would have to be an online degree. Next, the question was which online university would be widely recognized by hiring officials and was fully accredited and recognized by the US Department of Education. This requirement narrowed it down to two prospects. I finally decided upon one university because it not only provided an online environment but required at least three (3) residencies where I could meet fellow national and international students, faculty, and hone in and be exposed to my disciple. So, in late fall of 2006, I enrolled in my first doctoral program.

After being registered for the required course work toward my disciple, I found that the course work somewhat mimicked those of a Master's program but differed in the rigor and substantial "homework" research material. The demand for accuracy of the APA format was most pressing. The discussions required a more in-depth synthesis and evaluation of the subject matter. The word count requirement increased as time progressed. Completion of the required course work for my specialization took about one and half to two years to complete. Following the completion of the doctoral course work shadowed the first doctoral level challenge, the comprehensive exam (or "comps" for short) which was designed to evaluate my mastery and higher-order of thinking in my field of study.

The comprehensive exam consisted of at least three (3) research type questions in which the doctoral student had to answer each question in 12 to 15 pages, but cumulatively not to exceed 50 pages total. However, this requirement did not include references. If the doctoral student surpassed the page requirement, the reviewing committee would count up to 50 pages and discard the latter, which may result in responses not being coherent or incomplete, thereby, resulting in failure. Each doctoral student had at least one month to complete his or her comps after the completion of their doctoral course work.

Amina M. Abdullah-Winstead, PhD

Research Mentors or a Doctoral Comprehensive Examination Committee authored the comprehensive exam questions. Likewise, these questions were geared towards the student's specialization. Each student had at least two attempts to pass comps. If the student did not pass at the second attempt, they were dismissed from the university. At least three doctoral professors/researchers reviewed and evaluated responses. A doctoral student passed if the majority of the reviewers indicated that he or she provided adequate responses to at least two out of the three questions. If not, then a student failed. The latter happened to me. It was not clear on the reason for not advancing the first time but one thing was sure was the evidence of the disagreement among the reviewers whether it was a pass or fail.

On that day when I received and read my results that I had to attempt the comps again, I was disillusioned and livid. My Comps Mentor stated that most doctoral students do not pass their comps the first time around and that I should read the responses and implement the committee's suggestions. At the time, his words were not comforting. So, I took a long walk along the highway. I remember wearing a long ankle length dark blue casual dress and sandals. I walked about eight miles (maybe more) to clear my head. Living in central Florida at the time, the temperature was about 80 to 85 degrees Fahrenheit, but I was too driven to feel the heat.

I walked and I prayed. I prayed and I walked waiting to hear an answer from God. Hoping for a miracle and then it hit me. The sky opened and I found a clever way of re-writing my comps responses so that they would be accepted without changing the notion of my responses entirely. The challenge most doctoral students have is being passionate about a topic and having someone else tear it away from you or tell you it means nothing or that it will not amount to anything. Nevertheless, I prevailed and I passed my comps on the second attempt. Now, I was ready to select my mentor and dissertation committee and begin writing my dissertation.

During the doctoral course work, you were required to attend one Cohort where you met some potential mentors. It was there when I decided on my "first" mentor to guide me along my doctoral journey. Next, was to select my committee members. I chose two committee members who were well-versed in my topic interest and research methodology, which was quantitative. Prior to the approval of my committee members, I was told that I could not select a committee member outside of the university. So, both committee members were from my attending university.

Once my mentor and committee members were approved by the university, my mentor instructed me to send him my topic with at least three to five dissertation titles. Selecting a topic for my dissertation was easy because I was able to gather some ideas from my comprehensive exam. For some reason, I was drawn to the Dark Side of Leadership and as such fashioned my titles under this topic. More importantly, I was interested in the Dark Side of Leadership in both the Religious and Public Service sectors but fate would have its day.

Attending the residencies was one of the requirements towards the completion of the PhD. In the residencies, I discovered that it depends on how you formulate your research questions and what you want to know about your topic that determines the research methodology you should use. Well, there exits the question between completing a quantitative study or saying "hello" to qualitative methodology.

It was during this time that my dissertation journey began to stall. Each time I told my mentor what I wanted to study he would say do not attempt a qualitative study because it would take much longer to complete. I found his response to be untrue because my fellow colleagues, who completed a qualitative study, completed theirs within one to two years. Likewise, I have met some colleagues who attempted the quantitative methodology and completed theirs within three to four years. It all depends on your mentor and the committee and if they are willing to support your approach for your topic and methodology. Furthermore, I already invested time, money, and gathered all my research tools necessary for a qualitative study. Later, I began to get the impression that he was not comfortable with the qualitative methodology because each time I would contact him by email or phone, I would not hear back from him until a month or a month and half later. Here began my introduction to doctoral politics: The fight between which method is considered scientific; quantitative or qualitative.

Ten months had passed since completing my comps and my mentor was absent without leave (AWOL). I finally made the decision, realizing that time and money was wasting, to change my mentor. I reached out to a fellow doctoral colleague who highly recommended a hardworking and determined mentor. Following, I submitted my request for change to the university and it was approved. I had written my first three chapters (dissertation proposal) by the time I acquired my new mentor.

Once I was able to contact my new mentor, I asked him if we should also change the committee members since my previous mentor recommended them. At the time, he suggested not to change the members because he did not want to waste precious time. My new mentor assisted me with the completion of my dissertation proposal that we submitted and was approved on the first attempt. Then, a few weeks later, we got another notice that the proposal was not approved due to the chosen methodology. This notice was confusing because the first three chapters was approved which meant that the methodology was also approved. My mentor and I were back and forth with the school on why it was not approved. Better yet, it did not have a written reason beneath the rejection like other rejections normally displays, other than it was just not approved. Therefore, another six months of battle on the journey ensued.

As the probing commenced to find out why my proposal was not approved, the suggestions from Institutional Reviewing Board (IRB) were geared towards "turning" the study into a quantitative study rather than a qualitative study. Again, I began to wonder if everyone was afraid to attempt a qualitative study or was it possible that the dissertation reviewers did not understand or comprehend the qualitative methodology for my particular topic. The thought did cross my mind that it was a ploy by those concerned to show that it 'truly' does take an extensive amount of time to complete a "qualitative" study. Moreover, my method was new aged and was fashioned after new aged theoretical material from the university's published professors and completed dissertations as well as other well-known universities.

Nevertheless, about six months before I completed my

dissertation, the inevitable did occur which wasted more time. There was a change with the committee members because they too were more focused on the quantitative methodology rather than on the new direction of the dissertation, which was a qualitative methodology. This change, however, was different, as you will read in the following passages. Instead of me requesting the change, the school unilaterally made the decision.

The new committee suggested changes and I followed every direction only because I wanted to finish. Although, some of the changes were not clear or comprehensible, I completed each one nonetheless. Finally, the day came when we were ready to submit the revised dissertation proposal. Still, there was opposition but this time more on the side of doctoral "politics".

My doctoral political experience reminded me of the movie entitled "Dark Matter" starring Meryl Streep where she is a counselor to one foreign student enrolled in a doctoral program. The student whom she befriended was from China, she had a high IQ, and she was studying engineering. He studied the "dark matter" in space and discovered a new theory and a new method of studying space. He presented the idea to his mentor whom he lauded. However, rather than the mentor encouraging the student and work along with him, he disregards his theory and method all because he (the mentor) was not the first to discover it or exercise the possibilities.

In this scenario, the mentor used the Chinese student to complete difficult theories and equations while refraining to guide him through best practices; while at the same time considering the student and his Chinese colleagues to be "beneath him". When it came time to approve or disapprove the Chinese student's dissertation proposal, the mentor and "one" of the committee members rejects the dissertation proposal due to politics and past practice, while another colleague argues and agrees with the student that his discovery was profound and worth advancing for the benefit of science and new knowledge. Nevertheless, politics prevailed, and the "lords that be" rejected the student's dissertation. The movie is intriguing and unless you watch the movie in its entirety, you will not understand what doctoral students go through on their way to earning their PhD.

Despite the powers that be, fate would have it that I was granted favor from the Chair of Research and Analytics who inquired on why the process was taking so long for me to complete. The chairperson reviewed my paperwork to date and demanded a new committee and that I should continue where I left off (after the acceptance of my original proposal) so that I could advance to the next stage. My prayers were answered. This approval was all that I needed to complete my journey. Within three weeks, I completed field research, collected data, and wrote Chapter 4 and within one week evaluated, synthesized and wrote Chapter 5. My dissertation was complete. Now, I was ready for my dissertation defense. My defense entailed approximately 34 slides and was presented within 30 minutes with an additional 10 minutes for review and questioning. Having waited so long to come to that point, I was ready and passed my defense.

I gave much thought before answering one question my mentor asked me during my defense. He asked, "Having done what you have done and gone through, would you change anything or would you do things different?" My reply was, "No."

It was because of the challenges, upsets, disappointments, and setbacks that helped me prevail in this life-changing journey. It made me more humble, respectful, stronger, smarter, gifted, and clever. It pulled out of me what I thought never existed. I have indeed grown from this experience.

I was able to accomplish this feat while at the same time working as an college instructor and supporting one child still in college full time. Additionally, I faced personal struggles (cultural stereotypes, professional, and financial) during the process. Ironically, the cultural stereotypes affected me in my profession, which in turn affected the financial. The reason being, after arriving in Orlando in 2007, I found that I was second-guessed by the majority of interviewers. They made statements that implied that I "trumped" up my resume such as "...people from the Caribbean or the Virgin Islands live in trees and do not have an education higher than the 6th grade". Moreover, they certainly are not believed to have an IQ as high as 150. One interview, I will never forget, was with the Florida state/federal government. When the interviewer stated that it seems that I have "learned" the English language very well and asked how long did it take me to adapt to the American way of living. I was speechless as I realized the ignorance of the interviewers. I was shocked that people of well renowned professions and terminal degrees do not know world history or at least have sense enough to research someone's background for the validity of their claims or generalizations.

The US Virgin Islands' dominant language is English. The US Virgin Islands are a United States Territory as Puerto Rico is a common wealth. The other languages spoken are by immigrants who came from other islands. Any one born in the USVI after or subsequent to January 17, 1917 is considered a US Citizen and speaks English. The US Virgin Islands, and the Caribbean for that matter, birthed many movie stars, vocal artists, famous authors, statesmen, and athletes: Kelsey Grammer, Lawrence Hilton-Jacobs, Lisa Canning, Camille Pissarro (artist); Tim Duncan (basketball player); Emile Griffith (boxer); Julian Jackson (boxer); Sosthenes Behn (founder of ITT Cooperation); Alton Adams (musician - first black bandmaster in the United States Navy), just to name a few. I too believe I join the ranks of intriguing Virgin Islanders and will someday become a trailblazer to inspire others subsequent to this PhD journey.

The true PhD journey is a humbling experience. If you are not humble, you will become humble. If you believe that you have arrived or that you "know it all", then you have not taken the journey. Through this experience, I have learned politics and patience. I have learned to question outcomes and use hindrances as stepping stones towards the endgame to my ultimate victory. Thanks to the people who supported me throughout the process namely my mother, Judith, my Aunt Nettie, my cousin Delita, my pastors, and my children. Now, I am intrigued by research and new phenomenon. I see the bigger picture out of the smallest of things. I now understand and I am grateful for those who told me "no" when I wanted them to say "yes". I am wiser and now a seeker for new knowledge.

Renita L. Webb, Ph.D.

Happily, you will now embark on reading the journey of Dr. Renita L. Webb from start to Ph.D. My four year journey was full of turns and twists in my life path that encouraged my educational adventure. Though the road was not easy, I am thankful for each bump, slump, and dump that led me to encouragement, enlightenment, and fulfillment.

To provide you with a little background: I was born in North Carolina to the world's most powerful single mother ever, my story, and my opinion. My mother made sure that I was involved in a multitude of activities and supported me in them all while holding down multiple jobs. I was in church choir and dance starting at the age of two. Later I joined Girl Scouts, violin, cheerleading, student council, school chorus, additional dance classes, academic enrichment groups, and the church youth group. Even with all of these outside activities, my mother and I spent lots of time with family and close friends, who were just like family. For a long while I was the youngest child in my generation. There was a 12-year age difference between me my oldest cousin. According to them, I was the bossiest kid they had ever met. Who knew that the bossy trait would greatly help me in my future?

Though I never lived with my father, I knew him and until I was about 12, we had a decent relationship. Then there was a brief hiatus. But, my mother made sure that I never felt a lack of parental love and support. My uncle made sure that I always had a supportive and loving male figure in my life. Family friends also provided other positive and supportive males and females of all ages. They say it takes a village to raise a child and my village was grand.

As a child and throughout life I have always been an over achiever. I got straight A's until middle school and was devastated when I got a B in the sixth grade. I spent the day crying and afraid for my mother to find out. But, my mother showed me that it was NEVER about the grade, but that I always tried my best. But, for me I wanted as close to perfection as possible. I always thought that was there was more to do if I was not perfect or the best. In my activities, I met friends who were very like-minded. They would support my positive achievements and me theirs. Lots of them were surprisingly African American females. This is surprising because in African American culture there is lots of crab in a bucket syndrome, meaning that on occasion there can be a lack of support for those who are making an ascent upward in life.

By the time I reached high school, my main activity shifted to performing. I did school musicals, continued in church choir, and was involved in multiple choral groups at school. I was in the show choirs where I served as the lead choreographer for all choral groups my senior year. I was also a part of the countywide cabaret group that performed around the city and state, as well as a special performance for a governor's annual event. I knew that performing was what I wanted to do. I was selected to attend the state's governor's school summer program for choral music. During that summer, I constantly got sore throats and the doctor discovered I had vocal nodules. I had to endure a semester of vocal rest, speech therapy, and vocal lessons. This was a major test in my life, and I overcame. Please know that I did not do it alone. It was because of my faith in God, in the therapist, and the support that I received from my teachers, mentors, and family that helped me to endure. When that semester ended, I was back into performing full force. I was even selected to be the soloist for my high school graduation. Nevertheless, little did I know then that my life would soon veer away from performing on a stage to performance of a different sort.

While attaining my undergraduate degree, I went through changes and challenges. The biggest change was refocusing my major. I entered undergrad on a scholarship as vocal performance music major, but during my sophomore year, I had once again developed vocal nodules. It was at this time my voice teacher recommended that I start to think of another direction in school or risk the need for surgery or even permanent damage to my voice. Thus, I had to change my course. Since my mother told me that I had a total of four years of money to finish school and one and a half years were already gone, I had to figure out what major I could successfully finish in my remaining two and half years. This funding came from her job which paid for 80% of my tuition and the scholarships and grants I had earned. We did not have to pay for anything out of pocket except for my term abroad.

I switched to a major in English. While finishing this degree I served in several leadership positions on campus. I was a group president, a treasurer, an undergraduate teaching assistant, and a volunteer in the writing center. I also worked

5 jobs: 2 different restaurants, freelance choreography, substitute teaching, and in retail. I liked to shop and have a good time outside of class so I had to learn to like to work. I had to find the balance between work and play. My education still meant a great deal to me and I wanted my family to be proud of my successful completion of my undergraduate studies, even though I knew that my educational journey would not end there. Learning this balance would help me with my next two-degree studies.

Also during this time, my relationship with my father was revitalized. Upon reappearing in my life, I found that he had married. I love his wife. She is a strong woman who at the time seemed to play a part in his return. He began to help me financially, he became a greater presence, and he provided support. From that moment forward, our relationship has blossomed in to what most girls' dream of having with their father. I also gained a new woman in my life to assist in supporting and encouraging me.

After graduating with my first degree, I found myself doing what I planned never to do. I became a classroom teacher. My performing was relegated to teaching my students, coaching cheerleading, and singing for random events, weddings, and at church. Luckily, my drive never diminished. I found a friend, another African American woman, at my job that joined me in starting our next educational journey, the master's degree. We were recruited by a school representative for a college that was leaping into distance education for the first time.

We were intrigued and decided to give it a go. I started my M.Ed. program during my first year teaching. I attained my first real student loans to pay for the program. I plowed through the program, taking 2-3 classes at a time. I would type papers late into the night during the school year and any chance I got during the summers. I would even type during the breaks I had while working at two different summer music camps, giving my joy of performing to the future of the art. During this journey, I completed my first three years of teaching, which included a three-month hiatus from education and an additional six-month hiatus from the classroom. But, the Lord saw fit for me to return. During my third year of teaching and after completing my administrative internship, I realized that being a part of the education arena was affixed to my destiny.

I also completed my degree with a 3.8 GPA, I got a B in one class. I was frustrated that I was that close to perfection, but missed it by so little. I knew then that my move to administration was inevitable, though I would soon find out that my timing was not the timing in which I would be able to move into a new position. I interviewed for several positions just after completing my degree. I did not receive a new job. Thus, I returned to the classroom for another year. I was challenged to be my team lead even though I was only a fourth year teacher, the coordinator for a school program, and taught an elective during a portion of my planning period. I was proving that I could lead and withstand the pressures of the position that I was ready to attain. I also knew that eventually I would obtain my terminal degree. I challenged myself to get it, to have it, and prove that I could become a doctor.

Following my fourth year in the classroom, I was granted the position of assistant principal (AP). I was in this position when I met another African American woman who changed my life. It was my principal. She was near retirement, but had earned her doctoral degree in the later years of her career.

She encouraged me from day one, not to be comfortable with my M.Ed. she said that it was not common to have. If I wanted to move forward in my career, I would need to attain my doctoral degree. It was with that degree that I would stand out from the crowd in addition to doing dynamic work in my daily position. During my first year in the position, my principal saw fit to start grooming me for a principal-ship. She would put me in key positions and situations for me to gain the experience and foresight of a keen school administrator. It was also during this time that I decided to marry the man whom I started dating during my final year of teaching.

We married the summer after my first year as an AP, and I started my doctoral studies a month after our union. When I married my husband, I became a mother to two boys, 10 and 8-years old. Soon after our wedding, we discovered we were expecting our first child together. But, having all of this going on only compelled me to continue to achieve educational greatness. I would be the first in my family to attain a doctoral degree and I wanted all of them to be proud of me. I also wanted to be an example to my family, friends, and those children who looked up to me, that if you want something you would get it, no matter what.

I chose Capella University to get the degree because I had previously taken courses online and loved it. A good friend from my undergraduate studies completed her masters with Capella and spoke very highly of the schools rigorous curriculum, professional staff, and relevant application of study information. I was going to have to use loans once again to pay, because as a new family and having a husband that was in school full time, we could not afford the additional payments. However, I knew that having this new degree would eventually pay for itself, or at least I hoped it would.

Amina M. Abdullah-Winstead, PhD

A month after I started my doctoral studies, my husband and I found out we would not be having a live birth. Losing the baby was devastating, but I did not allow it to derail me from school. Placing more focus on my school work helped to distract me from losing the baby, though it did not make me forget. I also returned to work soon after my recovery. I had to keep moving forward. I continued classes as we continued to attempt to enlarge our family. I also challenged myself to get a 4.0 GPA in these studies. After receiving that one B during my masters studies, I knew that I could manage to get all A's. I wanted the 4.0 badly.

A few months later, we were pregnant again, things at work were getting more challenging, and my studies continued. I attended the required colloquiums which provided a great opportunity to network with the professors and classmates. It also helped to prepare me for my comprehensive exam (comps) and dissertation. It was from the colloquiums that I garnered a support network of my Capella peers that would keep me encouraged along the journey. I was in my final phase of classwork during my final trimester of pregnancy. I was completing my superintendent internship. I was interested in trying to stay on top of my game at work, constantly trying to gain different experiences and professional development to prepare to become a principal, and take part in the multi-facets of the life of a superintendent.

I never used my pregnancy as an excuse to slow down. I had a wonderful superintendent mentor who allowed me to experience the different capacities of a district leader. He appointed me to a position to represent the district during my internship and for the remaining time I worked in the district. The largest piece of advice I remember from him was not to allow the job to consume me. He advised me to take vacations when I could, which I still have not quite followed, but I will soon. He always encouraged me to keep striving and told me about the great job I was doing.

In my position as intern, I was also able to gain a deeper relationship with the assistant superintendents in the district. They would provide me with information about their positions and how they helped to keep the district running. They also became a support network for me in addition to a few other employees at the central office. Of course, while I was doing this internship, I was still working in the school as an assistant principal. Thankfully, my principal was one who was willing to allow me to do what I needed to in order to have a well-rounded internship experience. Soon after I completed my final leg of coursework, I gave birth to a beautiful baby girl. But, of course the next phase of my doctoral journey was on the horizon, the comprehensive exam.

Having just given birth before my comps and realizing that I would be out of work for six weeks, seemed to be the stage for inevitable success, but there was a bump in the road coming. When my daughter was three weeks old, I picked her up and she was not breathing. This was of course the week my comps were scheduled to start. Well, we rushed to the emergency room (ER) and found out that there was something going on with her and she was indeed having random moments she would stop breathing. We were at one hospital that did not have a strong pediatric department and we were moved to another hospital where we would be for the next two weeks.

During that time, my professor assured me that I did not need to complete my exam at that time and should take care of my family. But, while sitting in that hospital room 24 hours a day looking at my baby and realizing there was nothing I could do but be there to love her, I needed a distraction. My husband was at home with our sons, thus most of the time I was in the hospital alone, aside from visits from my mother, other family members, friends, and church supporters. For a portion of the time we were in the hospital's pediatric intensive care unit because my daughter was a code blue at one point in time. It was during that time that I requested my comprehensive exam, going against what my professor stated.

When we returned to the main floor, I would work on the comps whenever my daughter was sleeping, which was often. My husband bought my school books to the hospital. I would cry and type, type and cry. I would pray and sing worship songs. I would pump milk and feed my daughter when I could. We had great nurses and one particular doctor on rotation that would encourage me to keep working and they gave me the assurance that my daughter was in great hands. We had several success and setbacks, but typing helped to keep me distracted and the prayers kept me uplifted. I completed my comprehensive exam two days after my daughter was discharged and sent home with oxygen, a monitor, and medication to keep her breathing regularly. I found out a couple of weeks later that I passed my comps. I would also be on extended leave from work due to my daughter's illness. I did not return to work at the school until six and a half months later.

While I was on leave, my principal retired, my aunt came to North Carolina from Michigan to become our live-in full time nanny for a year, and I started working on my Scientific Merit Review (SMR – also known as a Research Study Plan/Proposal at some schools). I enjoyed getting to spend the extra time with my daughter. I was able to get donated leave from other state employees, thus I was paid for the entire time I was out of work. My husband and the boys helped whenever they could and they continued with school. My husband was supportive and loving throughout the entire experience; while he was experiencing his own challenges.

When I returned to work, it was a very different environment from the sense of family feeling that I left. The new administrator was in the business of change, there was a new second AP, and there were lots of disgruntled staff members. I was the only member of the administrative staff that was a part of the old regime. There was a new superintendent over the district, as my former mentor had also retired. I knew that it would not be long before I would need to make a transition. I continued during this time to work on my SMR, making correction after correction in attempts to get it approved. This was the hardest part of my doctoral journey. It is when I experienced the most rejection. It seemed as if there was nothing that I did absolutely correct.

For a perfectionist, this was very disheartening. So, I was going through some of my hardest times in my work life, motherhood (being separated from my daughter for the first time during the workday), and my doctoral journey at the same time. I am thankful that also at this time I discovered the Ph.D. Sisters group and another doctoral support group for women on Facebook. I know that most people would not think much of Facebook groups as a support network, but the ladies in these groups could speak to my experiences, they could accurately understand my complaints, and offer sound advice for advancement in the journey. These women allowed me to vent when I needed to and they celebrated my accomplishments big and small. While walking through this type of journey, having someone there to support you who can really understand what you are going through because they are either there or have been there, makes a world of difference.

Though I made a conscious effort to work on my chapters 1-3 while I was awaiting SMR approval, which took over a year, when it was time to really get into my dissertation work, time seemed to fly. I received a promotion and became the inaugural principal at an elementary charter school. I was able to hire my own staff, select school programs, and amend with the construction design. I was working an hour away from home with a one year old, a 12 year old, and a 14 year old. They were all active children. I was also writing my dissertation and trying to be a good wife. My husband had done his initial sermon less than six months before and I had just accepted my call into the ministry. The final year of my doctoral journey was guaranteed to be jam packed with excitement.

Five months later, I preached my initial sermon and became a licensed minister. Seven months after chapters 1-3 were completed and approved, I was approved by the School of Education and the IRB to collect my data. The data collection process was the best part of my dissertation journey. I was able to meet some incredible African American female educators who whether they wanted to advance or simply be the best at what they do, were positive influences in the field and making a major difference in the lives of children. The superintendents

I met encouraged me to keep moving forward in my career. They were happy to see a women so young embarking on this part of the journey.

It took me three months from the beginning of my data collection to the successful defense of my dissertation. It was like I blinked and it was suddenly all over. My defense experience proved that I really was a scholar and worthy of being in conversations with other doctors with years of experience. I realized that I was the expert on my research and I had something to bring to the table. When I graduated with distinction, because I achieved that 4.0 GPA, in Minneapolis, MN, I was so proud and felt a true sense of accomplishment. Having my mother and close family friend, who is just like an aunt to me, there at graduation made it all the more special. I had done something no one else in my family and few in my circle had achieved. I became an inspiration to others. I could influence the lives of other people by continuing to live mine in a positive way.

Having my new credential has caused some people to listen to more of what I have to say. Simply by having the title, I have gotten more respect from some of the parents and the other staff members at my school. I have been invited to be a part of publications like this one and others. I now have more job opportunities and chances for career growth or shift. I see a sense of pride in the eyes of those connected to my life. Not only because they are proud of me personally, but also because they are proud to see an African American young lady making positive achievements in life.

My goal was to be all but dissertation by the time I was 30, I achieved it by 29. So, today I am a 31 year old Ph.D.

holder, principal of an elementary school, minister, wife, and mother (the kids are now 2, 13, and 15). I am apart of several organizations and have been invited to hold positions on several boards since I obtained the degree. I will be using this degree as leverage to catapult myself into different arenas and levels of my career. I still am striving to be the best at what I do. I am now focusing on my ministerial studies, and I will start my Masters of Divinity degree within the month. I am also working on the art of research by networking and meeting others in my field and allowing my doctorate degree to open doors and start conversations to allow my ear to be in the room and my voice to be heard.

About The Editor

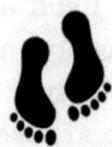

Dr. Amina Abdullah-Winstead holds a PhD in Human Services from Capella University and a Master's degree in Management from University of Phoenix in Management. She is a Lead Faculty for the Human Services program at Saint Leo University in the Virginia Peninsula, the President of the International PhD Sisters Association (IPSA) and founder of the PhD Sisters Support Group on Facebook in addition to the Pi Eta Delta Sorority. She has over twenty years of combined, professional experience from positions held in academia, telecommunications, health care, and health insurance.

Connect with a support group:

International PhD Sisters Association (IPSA)
www.phdsisters.com

Pi Eta Delta Sorority (PED)
www.pietadelta.com

PhD Sisters Support Group (PSSG)
https://www.facebook.com/groups/phdsisters

Amazon Author Page
http://amzn.com/e/B009FQ7UK8

www.ingramcontent.com/pod-product-compliance
Lightning Source LLC
LaVergne TN
LVHW052256070426
835507LV00035B/3074